SERIOUS

COMIX

ENGAGING STUDENTS WITH DIGITAL STORYBOARDS

Eydie Wilson

International Society for Technology in Education
EUGENE, OREGON • WASHINGTON, DC

Serious Comix
Engaging Students with Digital Storyboards
Eydie Wilson

Director of Book Publishing: *Courtney Burkholder*
Acquisitions Editor: *Jeff V. Bolkan*
Developmental Editor: *Mike van Mantgem*
Production Editors: *Lynda Gansel, Tina Wells*
Production Coordinator: *Emily Reed*
Graphic Designer: *Signe Landin*
Copy Editor: *Kärstin Painter*
Cover Design, Book Design, and Production: *Gwen Thomsen Rhoads*

First Edition
ISBN: 978-1-56484-321-0 (paperback)
ISBN: 978-1-56484-475-0 (e-book)
Printed in the United States of America

Cover and inside art by author's students Brock and Stewie
ISTE® is a registered trademark of the International Society for
Technology in Education.

SUSTAINABLE FORESTRY INITIATIVE
Label applies to the text stock

Certified Sourcing
www.sfiprogram.org
SFI-00341

About ISTE

The International Society for Technology in Education (ISTE) is the trusted source for professional development, knowledge generation, advocacy, and leadership for innovation. ISTE is the premier membership association for educators and education leaders engaged in improving teaching and learning by advancing the effective use of technology in PK–12 and teacher education.

Home to ISTE's annual conference and exposition and the widely adopted NETS, ISTE represents more than 100,000 professionals worldwide. We support our members with information, networking opportunities, and guidance as they face the challenge of transforming education. To find out more about these and other ISTE initiatives, visit our website at www.iste.org.

As part of our mission, ISTE Book Publishing works with experienced educators to develop and produce practical resources for classroom teachers, teacher educators, and technology leaders. Every manuscript we select for publication is carefully peer-reviewed and professionally edited. We value your feedback on this book and other ISTE products. Email us at books@iste.org.

International Society for Technology in Education
Washington, DC, Office:
    1710 Rhode Island Ave. NW, Suite 900, Washington, DC 20036-3132
Eugene, Oregon, Office:
    180 West 8th Ave., Suite 300, Eugene, OR 97401-2916
Order Desk: 1.800.336.5191
Order Fax: 1.541.302.3778
Customer Service: orders@iste.org
Book Publishing: books@iste.org
Book Sales and Marketing: booksmarketing@iste.org
Web: www.iste.org

About the Author

Eydie Wilson holds a doctorate in philosophy from the Graduate Center of the City University of New York. She has a master's degree and a bachelor's degree in computer science and information systems. Wilson works as an adjunct professor in both the Math and Computer Science Departments and the Departments of Counseling, Leadership, Literacy, and Special Education at Lehman College, the City University of New York. A former district math coach for middle and high school teachers, she is now school-based as a coach and mentor in the New York City Department of Education. She also serves as a mentor to struggling students. Her research focuses on differentiated teaching strategies and the integration of technology as a tool across subjects.

Contents

Preface vii

Introduction 1

Chapter 1
Encouraging Literacy, Embracing Technology 7
    What is Serious Comix? 9
    Comics and Literacy 10
    Technology as Instructional Tool 13
    The Learning Environment 13
    Technology Standards and Teacher Knowledge 14
    Concluding Thoughts 19

Chapter 2
Designing the Learning Environment 21
    Student-Centered Instructional Cycle 22
    Cogenerative Dialog Format 24
    Classroom Layout 32
    Encouraging Peer-to-Peer Dialogue 33

Chapter 3
Student Ownership of Learning 35
    Triggering the Skills Transfer 36
    A New Classroom Culture 37
    Peer Tutoring 37
    Positive Environment 40

Chapter 4
Creating Serious Comix: Foundations 43
    Foundations for Building Literacy 44
    Foundations for Technology Learning 49
    Software Applications 54
    Publishing for Presentation 56

Chapter 5
Reflections 59

Serious Comix Lesson Plans 63

    Lesson 1: Introduction to Comic Books,
        Technology Tools, and Cogenerative Dialogue 68

    Lesson 2: Story Writing and Illustration Creation Using
        Graphic Organizers, Part I 71

    Lesson 3: Story Writing and Illustration Creation Using
        Graphic Organizers, Part II. 74

    Lesson 4: Scanning Illustrations to Digital Format 76

    Lesson 5: Creating Digital Comic Books in PowerPoint 78

    Lesson 6: Presenting Digital Comic Book to Peers. 80

Appendix A
Special Education in New York City 83

Appendix B
Resources for Educators 90

References 93

Preface

The Serious Comix project was born from my graduate studies research proposal, which had the premise of using technologically mediated instruction to improve literacy skills. My goal for the project was to enhance the way students access and retain literacy skills by integrating technology as an instructional tool. I knew I needed to tailor the program to the students I would be working with—a small, voluntary group of special education students in an urban middle school. But although my instructional planning was focused on that particular group of students, it was based on strong foundational theory that can be applied to many different educational situations.

My choice of digital storyboarding as the instructional strategy was strongly influenced by two things. The first was information I gathered by attending Media: Overseas Conversation (IV): An International Conference on Media Literacy-Ecology-Studies Education. Over the course of the conference, I listened to proponents for and opponents of technology in education. Of particular interest to me were those who saw technology, when used properly as an academic tool, as a vehicle to close achievement gaps and offer equity.

Urban, poor students assigned to disability status are very often faced with issues of digital equity because they do not have the same exposure to technology as their general education counterparts, nor do they share the same knowledge of how technology relates to learning. Thus, I felt strongly that my project should use technology as an instructional tool.

The second influence was my desire to practice alternative, student-centered teaching strategies because I felt that they could positively affect the learning environment and the teaching experience. This desire was reinforced by the recommendation from the International Reading Association (2000) that teachers be responsible for finding and using alternative teaching strategies to address learning and transform education.

I knew that to create a successful program, I would need to analyze the educational policies under which I would be working, my own personal stereotypes of technology, and the academic abilities and expectations of the special education students in my school.

INTRODUCTION

The reasonable man adapts himself to the world; the
unreasonable one persists in trying to adapt the world
to himself. Therefore, all progress depends on the
unreasonable man.

—George Bernard Shaw 1856–1950

I worked anxiously in my hot, cramped office at my oversized
desk, trying to finish the six-week schedule for Serious Comix, a
project designed to promote achievement in literacy, when I noticed
it was time to go to class. As two copies of the schedule printed
(one for myself and one for the lab teacher), I contemplated my
plans for teaching my group of District 75 (D75) students at PS/MS
South Bronx, an elementary and secondary special education school
(Grades K–8).

In the New York City Department of Education, D75 is the citywide
self-contained division for students who have been classified with
disabilities that affect learning (see Appendix A for further details
about the special education system in New York City). In the South
Bronx, a notoriously tough neighborhood, the term *disabilities* has
many attributes. Officially, my students had personal disabilities that
prevented them from satisfactory academic achievement in a regular
classroom. But the persistent challenges that my students encountered on a daily basis beyond the classroom, such as poverty, illness,

lack of educational role models, low parental interest, and unsteady home lives, hindered them with multiple challenges that are known to have a negative impact the educational lives and academic results of many urban students (Wilson, 1996).

In education, segregation by disability is known as *self-containment.* Common challenges of students in self-contained environments that affect both reading and writing are absenteeism and problems with attention, memory, and organization (Bay & Bryan, 1992). Statistics provided by the Bureau of Justice (Coley & Barton, 2006) reported at least 68% of the incarcerated population does not have a high school diploma and the survey conducted demonstrated a high percentage of illiterate members. Drakeford (2003) highlights the correlations between illiteracy and high crime, poverty, and ill health in urban areas. Barton and Jenkins (1995) also found that the trajectory for such impoverished individuals is often incarceration. This makes literacy of paramount importance to these disadvantaged students.

Schedules in hand, I paused to recheck the package that I planned to take to the computer lab: handheld video recorder, batteries, work folder, pencils, paper, colored pencils, storage media, and a copy of a comic book. I had at my disposal the essential tools that, in conjunction with detailed strategies to promote achievement in literacy, would help each student create a simple comic book. More than that—a serious work of his or her own design. My detailed schedule included meeting days and times (the voluntary project ran concurrently with students' existing class schedules), as well as instructional plans for introducing and teaching new technology applications and for providing writing time, review, and discussion. This pause also gave me a moment to mull over the difficulty I would likely encounter in trying to convene the student participants, with their differing schedules and individual challenges, into the cohesive, functioning group I envisioned. I had to overcome an educational system that required students to navigate through elaborate institutional rules, constraints, and lunch schedules. And now it was time to start the class.

Over the six weeks of the Serious Comix project, the students who had chosen to participate would work on their literacy skills and technology skills by each creating a comic book of his or her own. They would explore the reading, writing, and visual design processes and learn the terminology associated with them. To facilitate their learning, we would focus on the most efficient and effective technological applications. Students would learn how to navigate the computer desktop environment; scan artwork; and use Microsoft applications to create storylines, manipulate scanned images, and publish storyboards, while simultaneously learning basic technological terms.

I grabbed a cold bottle of water from my fridge, picked up my keys, shut off my monitor, and flicked off the light, then closed and locked the door with a parting thought: This was going to be a lot of work. Could these kids handle it? Could I?

My anxiety fell away when I entered the computer lab. My school had provided me with dedicated access to its fourth-floor computer lab once a week during lunch. I had also made arrangements to ensure that students could use the computer lab during the last periods of the day to work on their comic books.

The lab was split into two sections—12 to 14 desk-chair combinations to facilitate discussions and simple instructions on one side, and 12 to 14 individual computer terminals on the other side. This arrangement was designed to foster the type of engaging classroom experience I wanted for the students. I knew that the hardware and programs I needed were ready and available. There was an interactive whiteboard, two working printers, and a scanner, and the outdated but functional personal computers were loaded with older versions of Microsoft Word and PowerPoint.

In arranging the computer lab for the Serious Comix students, I created a physical space meant to encourage students to engage in free and open dialogue. Here they could see one another's facial expressions, talk without raising hands, explore the environment, and engage with others in ways not usually permitted in a formal classroom. These are all important components of the cogenerative dialogue instructional method, a format that would become an important part of my work with the students (see Chapter 2 for a full discussion). I was introduced to cogenerative dialogue during my doctoral studies in education by my professor and advisor, Kenneth Tobin. He worked extensively with disadvantaged urban students—general education students with lives similar to those of my students—though my students had the added complexity of being assigned a disability status.

Thoughts about instructional style had led me to consider my ability to integrate technologically mediated instruction. I wanted to present content in a coherent, logical, and accessible manner. As a D75 teacher, I knew my self-contained urban students, who were classified as having various disabilities and who were also academically, socially, and financially disadvantaged, faced issues of inequity because they did not have the same exposures to technology (updated equipment; school or home access) as did their general education counterparts. More importantly, they did not share the same knowledge of how technology related to learning. I felt that some of these hindrances to technological equity could be traced to teachers' lack of technology skills and training—in my school I had noticed teachers using the computer simply as a behavior management device, rewarding unruly students who temporarily exhibited good behavior with time to play games or watch videos. In this sense, computers and technology had become toys to distract and reward rather than tools that could be used to acquire knowledge, enhance literacy skills and learning, or research academic topics of interest. My choice of using technology and comics in order to foster student literacy was no accident. With the Serious Comix project, I hoped to connect the fun and engaging nature of both computers and comic books with real learning and the enhancement of each student's literacy skills.

Teachers must recognize that capturing student attention is essential to learning. At the cusp of the 21st century, the International Reading Association (2000) stated that teachers are responsible for finding and using alternative teaching strategies to address learning and transform the classroom. The Common Core State Standards in English language arts call for students to use technology, including the Internet, to produce and publish writing, as well as to interact and collaborate with others. The Common Core State Standards aim to integrate technology and multimedia into all daily academic subjects. Although there are many ways to fuse English language arts and technology into teaching and learning, using comic books (and variations such as storyboards or graphic novels) has become popular in the classroom because of comic books' popularity across student populations. Comic books are inherently attention-grabbing.

I completed my preparation for class as the bell rang and the students appeared. I soon met Brock and Stewie, whose educational journeys—from an interest in comics to a real interest in technology and school—you will read about throughout the book. Despite the environment in which they lived, despite the labels they carried, they were able to reconstruct their identities as learners. Through the Serious Comix project, they began to see themselves as members of a community that progressed by adapting technology to meet their learning needs in a meaningful way.

Chapter 1

ENCOURAGING LITERACY, EMBRACING TECHNOLOGY

S erious Comix is a student-centered literacy-building program in which students use technology to create and present their own digital comic books (digital storyboards). Students enhance their reading/writing and visual literacy skills and learn transferrable technology skills while working in an environment created to support dialogue and collaboration.

To create a Serious Comix digital storyboard, students engage in a combination of reading, writing, and image creation within a comic-strip–style format. Students find the comic book format easy to understand and use. Because comic books are laid out in sequential frames, it is easy for readers to track the progress of a story. The format also allows student authors to easily jump ahead and go back as necessary during the creative process. Because each frame contains both text and a picture, readers can easily grasp and contextualize a story, and writers are not overwhelmed by the amount of text they need to produce. Moreover, the clearly defined framing and sequencing of a comic helps students better understand the critical literary points of a story.

Serious Comix is a fun and engaging project. Students are excited at the thought of creating their own comic books. But students aren't simply assigned to draw a cartoon. Serious Comix invites students to organize their thoughts. Through guided practice, students are shown how to give structure to their ideas and how to commit those ideas to writing and illustrations via the use of graphic organizers.

The comic book creation process has three essential components: the dialogue exchange, the writing process, and the use of technology to construct and present the comic book. These components are combined into teaching and learning activities such as discussing and developing story ideas, learning and using graphic organizers, working independently and as part of a team, evaluating the work of peers, using technology as a tool to complete work, and presenting the finished product. Class time is designed to allow students to share stories and ideas, improve literacy and technology skills, and interact with each other.

What Is Serious Comix?

As I developed the Serious Comix project, I encountered some fundamental instructional, technological, and environmental concerns. Answering the following questions helped me fuse my knowledge of technology, curriculum mandates, and student dispositions into the whole that is Serious Comix.

> *Digital Storyboards and Literacy.* What sort of comic will students create? How will this activity meet the literacy development needs of diverse learners? How does the creation of this comic address the integration of literacy and technology?

> *Technology as Instructional Tool.* What is meant by "technology as an instructional tool"? How should technology be used as an instructional tool?

> *Teaching and Learning Environment.* How can the teaching environment foster reflective practices and ongoing assessments that are specific to both technology integration and literacy? What are the key characteristics that inform instructional planning in a nontraditional or alternative environment?

> *Technology Standards and Teacher Knowledge.* What are the technology standards for teaching literacy and technology? How will the technological knowledge and skills of a classroom teacher affect technology integration within the larger literacy curriculum?

Comics and Literacy

Benjamin Franklin's newspaper, the *Pennsylvania Gazette*, published one of the earliest comics that included situation, text, and cartoon characters. On May 9, 1754, the famous "Join, or Die" cartoon appeared (see Figure 1.1). It was a call for the original colonies to unite in the common cause of rebellion against English rule, and it is considered to be the first American political cartoon. That we remember it today is testament to the enduring power of Franklin's creative imagination, technical skill, and political vision. It is also a testament to the power of blending images with text—readers in Franklin's time readily understood the message and intent of this cartoon, just as readily as we do today.

Figure 1.1 Comics blend image with text to create meaning

This connection between words and illustrations—whether encountered in cartoons, comic strips, comic books, or graphic novels—can transform the way we read. First thought of as just an amusement or distraction, comics have found a legitimate place in the classroom. There are two main advantages of using digital storyboards for improving literacy. The first is that research has shown that the use of comic books as instructional texts has a positive impact on improving students' literacy skills (Starr, 2004). Creating and interpreting images also enables students to access higher-order creative and critical thinking skills (Bloom, 1984). The second is that using images to facilitate reading and writing is a form of differentiated instruction that expands student access to the classroom English language arts curriculum. Viewing a storyboard, students are able to analyze images in order to sequence, decode, comprehend, and infer the storyline (Piro, 2002). In this way, comics can provide entry points, learning tasks, and outcomes that can meet diverse student literacy needs.

Although Serious Comix students may not create digital storyboards with a relevance that will span generations, their creations nonetheless will, in some way, share a common visual language, organizational sensibility, and presentation style with Franklin's classic work. More importantly, a student's digital storyboard will demonstrate individual interests and purpose and will provide tangible evidence of individual growth in terms of literacy and effective technology use.

Promoting Multiple Literacies

Literacy is more than the ability to read and write. The United Nations Educational, Scientific and Cultural Organization (UNESCO) defines *literacy* as the "ability to identify, understand, interpret, create, communicate, compute, and use printed and written materials associated with varying contexts. The development of literacy involves a continuum of learning in enabling individuals to achieve their goals, to develop their knowledge and potential, and to participate fully in their community and wider society." The word *literacy* has been attached to math, science, social studies, media, and now technology.

Schools everywhere are tasked with increasing traditional literacy levels. For example, as of 2003, New York City's public schools were mandated to teach a "Balanced Literacy" curriculum. According to the curriculum, students must be immersed and exposed to a literature-rich environment for all subjects (e.g., classroom libraries, wall words, posters, bulletin boards, and other like items). The New York City Department of Education website (http://schools.nyc. gov) discusses how Balanced Literacy is implemented in each class as it "stresses the essential dimensions of reading through explicit teaching of phonics, phonemic awareness, fluency and expressiveness, vocabulary, and comprehension. Daily read-aloud, independent reading time, reading workshop, writing workshop, and systematic word study instruction are key features of the approach."

The Serious Comix project promotes traditional literacy, visual literacy, and technology literacy. Students learn to improve their reading and writing skills by connecting created images and text. The students' ability to create a storyline—reading and writing, analyzing and comprehending words—is a strong and relevant foundation from which to teach literacy strategies. Technology literacy is accomplished through the use of instructional tools such as word processors and presentation applications.

Visual Literacy

According to Arizpe (2001), creating and interpreting images enables students to develop their visual literacy skills. Visual literacy skills allow students to analyze their images, express their thoughts verbally, and then associate text in the form of a storyline. In Serious Comix, graphic organizers are used as an instructional tool to bridge traditional and visual literacy.

Graphic organizers (visual learning aids that can represent knowledge, concepts, or ideas in an organized manner) are used to facilitate the introduction of visual storytelling issues that may be new to students while allowing teachers to review the primary elements of a story (main idea, beginning, middle, and conclusion) that students may already have encountered elsewhere. Teachers can use graphic organizers to integrate visual storytelling language basics into their lessons.

Technology as Instructional Tool

One of the primary goals of the Serious Comix project is the development of beginning technology literacy. The use of technology as a literacy instructional tool often appears to motivate struggling students to spend more time practicing important academic skills (Daiute, 1983). Digital technology is a particularly effective tool for helping students to create comics. This technology offers a predictable, forgiving workspace and provides the students an open yet controlled environment in which to explore their ideas.

My technology-literacy schedule for instructional planning and delivery is focused on the student's individual needs. This is to say, in some ways each Serious Comix project is custom built for its particular students. I believe the goals of integrating technology as a tool for literacy must be aligned with the following:

- Acknowledging that a student does not come to school as a blank slate, but has a culturally specific set of tools that should be used to facilitate learning.

- Knowing how each student learns and taking into consideration the specific strengths and weaknesses of each student.

- Recognizing that we (teacher–student or student–student) will learn from each other, both individually and collectively, about technology, literacy skills, and learning strategies.

The Learning Environment

Social interaction is a critical component of learning and one major aspect of social interaction is talking, or dialogues. I designed the learning environment of the Serious Comix class to encourage dialogue—both between student and teacher and between student and student—enabling students to discuss what and how they are learning. According to Mink (1988), students can make a personal connection to their academics and will be more inclined to retain information when provided an opportunity to discuss it.

This instructional method is based on Tobin and Roth's (2006) work on cogenerative dialogue. This method provides a way for students and teachers to distinguish a formal classroom setting from an "alternative" setting, thereby creating a space where all participants can imagine, share, and envision together what is possible outside the traditional classroom. This format allows the free production of newly acquired cultures (e.g., talking without raising hands, exploring the environment), which help students explore and practice literacy skills and technology. I will discuss cogenerative dialogue in more detail in Chapter 2.

In my own experience with Serious Comix, I found that the dialogue format put students at ease because it eliminated the fear of being put on the spot to "correctly" answer a question. The use of open dialogue enabled the students to relax and learn technology and literacy at their own pace. The cogenerative dialogue learning environment helped participants explore their ideas, opinions, and feelings and assist one another through sharing and questioning in a measured, step-by-step learning process. This environment also expanded the power to act for all participants, resulting in more opportunities for peer teaching .

Technology Standards and Teacher Knowledge

The process of creating storyboards for the Serious Comix project requires students to use technology applications and puts demands on their existing literacy skills. But because the focus of Serious Comix is literacy development, once the students learn the technology involved, the technology itself needs to fade into the background. And it is the quality of the instructor-created learning environment that ultimately determines the extent of this technology integration.

Good instruction is critical in helping students to make effective use of technologies. This is true of any tool, from pencil and paper to computers and interactive whiteboards. It is the extent to which instructional strategies effectively incorporate technology that affects student success in terms of meaningful storyboard creation. I recommend basing instructional design on national and regional standards.

ISTE's NETS

The 21st century was ushered in by significant changes to educational policy in regard to technology instruction. First, there was the signing of the No Child Left Behind Act of 2001 (NCLB), which became the guiding educational legislation of the land, causing a 2004 revision of the Individuals with Disabilities Education Act (IDEA). This revision aligned the NCLB and IDEA by highlighting technology as a tool that is capable of enhancing academics and closing achievement gaps. NCLB further asserted that "highly qualified" teachers are individuals who are capable of integrating technology as an academic tool into the curriculum to improve student achievement (NCLB, 2001).

Based on NCLB and IDEA, teachers are mandated to prepare the student population academically, with the use of technology as an instructional tool for the changing educational, technological, and economic world.

This mandate for technology integration is supported by policymakers at all levels and is promoted by organizations such as the National Council for Accreditation of Teacher Education (NCATE) and the International Society for Technology in Education (ISTE). ISTE, in partnership with others, developed educational technology standards for four different groups of users:

- NETS•S for students

- NETS•T for teachers

- NETS•A for administrators

- NETS•C for technology coaches

Instructional design for Serious Comix is based on ISTE's educational technology standards NETS•S and NETS•T. These standards identify "highly qualified" teachers as those who, among other things, learn and apply strategies using technology to support learners with diverse needs and backgrounds.

ISTE's NETS for Students (NETS•S)

The NETS•S states that all K–12 students should be prepared to meet the following standards and performance indicators.

1. **Creativity and Innovation**
   Students demonstrate creative thinking, construct knowledge, and develop innovative products and processes using technology.

2. **Communication and Collaboration**
   Students use digital media and environments to communicate and work collaboratively, including at a distance, to support individual learning and contribute to the learning of others.

3. **Research and Information Fluency**
   Students apply digital tools to gather, evaluate, and use information.

4. **Critical Thinking, Problem Solving, and Decision Making**
   Students use critical-thinking skills to plan and conduct research, manage projects, solve problems, and make informed decisions using appropriate digital tools and resources.

5. **Digital Citizenship**
   Students understand human, cultural, and societal issues
   related to technology and practice legal and ethical behavior.

6. **Technology Operations and Concepts**
   Students demonstrate a sound understanding of technology
   concepts, systems, and operations.

   © 2007 International Society for Technology in Education (ISTE), www.iste.org

ISTE's NETS for Teachers (NETS•T)

The NETS•T states that all classroom teachers should be prepared to
meet the following standards and performance indicators.

1. **Facilitate and Inspire Student Learning and Creativity**
   Teachers use their knowledge of subject matter, teaching and
   learning, and technology to facilitate experiences that advance
   student learning, creativity, and innovation in both face-to-
   face and virtual environments.

2. **Design and Develop Digital-Age Learning Experiences and
   Assessments**
   Teachers design, develop, and evaluate authentic learning
   experiences and assessments incorporating contemporary
   tools and resources to maximize content learning in context
   and to develop the knowledge, skills, and attitudes identified
   in the NETS•S.

3. **Model Digital-Age Work and Learning**
   Teachers exhibit knowledge, skills, and work processes repre-
   sentative of an innovative professional in a global and digital
   society.

4. **Promote and Model Digital Citizenship and Responsibility**
   Teachers understand local and global societal issues and
   responsibilities in an evolving digital culture and exhibit legal
   and ethical behavior in their professional practices.

5. **Engage in Professional Growth and Leadership**
   Teachers continuously improve their professional practice, model lifelong learning, and exhibit leadership in their school and professional community by promoting and demonstrating the effective use of digital tools and resources.

© 2008 International Society for Technology in Education (ISTE), www.iste.org

Common Core State Standards Initiative

In 2009, the newest introduction to the U.S. educational arena was the Common Core State Standards (CCSS) Initiative, which aimed at preparing all students, to the best of their abilities, for college and/or careers (www.corestandards.org). The new standards were a joint effort among several agencies across the country to develop a set of rigorous and internationally competitive standards in English language and mathematics that included higher-order thinking and analytical skills for K–12, with a focus on successful postsecondary outcome. Competitive federal "Race to the Top" grants were provided as incentives to states that adopted the standards or similar internationally benchmarked standards and assessments that prepare students for success in college and the workplace.

In a press release dated July 2009, President Obama and U.S. Secretary of Education Arne Duncan announced a $4.35 billion Race to the Top grant program with a total pledge of $10 billion (www2. ed.gov/programs/racetothetop). The grants are designed to facilitate competition to spur innovation and reform in state and local-district K–12 education. States are awarded points for satisfying certain educational policies, such as improving teacher and principal effectiveness based on performance, demonstrating significant progress in raising achievement and closing gaps, and turning around the lowest achieving schools. In addition to the 485 possible points listed in the criteria, schools can earn an additonal 15 points if they meet the STEM (science, technology, engineering, and math) criteria.

On July 19, 2010, New York State offcically adopted the Common Core State Standards with full implementation expected by 2015. Based on the CCSS, the goal of English language arts is to ensure that students are suffciently prepared by the end of high school. This includes the key areas of reading, writing, language, speaking and listening, and technology viewed as a way to learn knowledge and skills in all subject areas. And, of course, with the implementation of new academic standards come new assessment benchmarks to measure student achievement. Formal assessment is expected to begin in the school year 2014–2015, which coincides with the projected implementation year for most states.

Concluding Thoughts

It is imperative for educators to have an arsenal of instructional alternatives to address different learning challenges, and to know how to administer them effectively. In this book, I intend to show you how the engagement created by the trifecta of comic book creation, access to technology tools, and a cogenerative dialogue classroom format leads to literacy gains for even the most challenged learners. Even better, the Serious Comix project instills a new level of agency in learners—a personal ownership of learning that more traditional lessons are not able to tap. Read on to learn more!

Chapter 2

DESIGNING THE LEARNING ENVIRONMENT

A s I planned the Serious Comix project, my first thoughts were that I did not want the sessions to feel like a typical classroom, with only teacher-led instruction.

After carefully considering how I was going to integrate technologically mediated instruction, I chose a student-centered instructional cycle that presents the content in a coherent, logical, and accessible manner; allows differentiated student assessment strategies; and encourages teacher reflection.

The cogenerative dialogue format was also an important part of the classroom. It was important that we (teacher and students) understood the learning environment as a place we created and defined together—a place where we all could feel comfortable, free, and without pressure while we discussed our work. This learning environment would enable us to understand each other and enable the students to take their learning back to their regular classrooms.

Student-Centered Instructional Cycle

When preparing to deliver a Serious Comix lesson, it is important to consider the role of technology in terms of literacy development for students. I recommend that planning adhere to ISTE technology standards, your particular state's standards (in my case, the NYS ELA standards), and the cogenerative dialogue format. In addition, I would argue that the most important element to consider is student learning. A student-centered instructional cycle is required to bring these elements together in order to optimize teaching and learning outcomes.

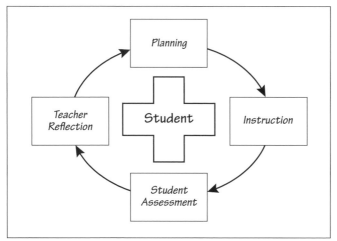

Figure 2.1 Serious Comix Technology-Literacy Instructional Cycle

Serious Comix's instructional cycle is a recursive plan with inter-locking, dependent elements that effectively addresses student learning (Figure 2.1). The instructional cycle includes the following components: planning for technology integration; meaningful instruction; assessment of student learning; and reflection on teaching and learning to make appropriate changes.

Planning for Technology Integration. The development of student literacy and technology skills should be taken into consider-ation in planning all phases of the cycle. Because too much information can overwhelm students and make the instruc-tion appear disjointed and unfocused, it is essential to create weekly lesson plans that present the tools for learning (e.g., graphic organizers, interactive whiteboard) at the appropriate stage. The lesson plans I created can be found starting on page 63.

Instruction. Implementing focused lesson plans is essential to scaffolding the weekly instructions. Teachers should model the appropriate use of learning tools. When teachers demonstrate and explain new tools and technologies, students are then able to use them competently and effectively.

Student Assessment. Based on direct observation of activity, student dialogue, or production of work based on lesson plan objectives, teachers must determine to what degree a student is or is not learning. Teachers must be able to identify and understand the strengths and weaknesses of a student.

Teacher Reflection. While assessing student achievements and weaknesses, teachers must also reflect what content was delivered and how it was presented. This reflection should inform the planning and instruction elements of the cycle.

Cogenerative Dialogue Format

The school environment can be somewhat tense, particularly with the focus on the Race to the Top, regulated settings, and changing policies and standards. Faced with this situation, schools tend to cling to traditional teaching methods and formal classrooms. However, I didn't think this was the best environment for learning technology. I wanted a more effective learning culture for my students—one in which they could freely discuss their ideas, learn new technology, help each other, and embrace learning. To help me achieve this, I turned to Roth and Tobin's (2004) ideas about cogenerative dialogue.

A simple definition of *cogenerative dialogue* is respectful interactions (dialogue) among participants where the goal is co-creating (cogenerating) a plan of action to improve future experiences. Cogenerative dialogue creates a space where discourse between teachers and students occurs without judgment (Tobin & Roth, 2006). Cogenerative dialogue helps teachers and students to create a safe and respected gathering area to discuss ideas, share information and opinions, and reflect on classroom teaching and learning experiences. Students are fully able to share their perspectives, which enables everyone participating to identify issues and contradictions that can be addressed to improve the environment. Everyone shares the responsibility to enact cultural, teaching, and learning changes.

What did cogenerative dialogue look like in the Serious Comix classroom? Students were instructed to show respect to and listen carefully to one another. Students were allowed to talk without raising their hands and able to explore the environment as long as they were respectful of their fellow students and the equipment. Peer interactions became an important part of student learning.

Six Characteristics of the Dialogue Format

When I plan to instruct technology and literacy using the cogenerative dialogue method, I am mindful of six primary characteristics:

1. Dialogue as instructional method

2. Time for critical thinking

3. Learning to learn avocation

4. Social interaction and collaboration

5. Access to technology, instructor, each other

6. Differentiation of instruction and one-to-one coaching

Dialogue as Instructional Method

I began Serious Comix by introducing the dialogue instructional method to the students. At the beginning of the first session, I described how the class would function, and I emphasized that it would be very different from a regular classroom. I stressed to students that because this was a voluntary program, their level of participation would be up to them, and they would not be subject to my grading or judgment. However, I explained that even though they would not be graded on their work, they still had a goal— improved literacy through the use of technology. To ensure that we all would have the best experience possible, I explained that everyone would have to follow certain parameters. For example, students would not have to raise their hands to comment or speak, but they must listen to each individual speaker. Students were free to move about and explore their environment, but they must respect the computers, the setting, and each other.

Time for Critical Thinking

Providing students with time to think and reflect is crucial for helping them learn. This "think time" allows the students to gather and organize new material and resolve conflicts. This process is the definition of critical thinking. Gunning (2003) asserts that critical thinking includes questioning information and developing multiple perspectives. It is important to understand that Serious Comix involves a social space within which all participants should feel comfortable and free—where students have more volition in the production of their work.

Unless they also offer students strategies for how to think, teachers who allow "think time" might very well be providing little more than "stare off into space time." Teachers must model how students should engage in critical thinking activities. Rowe (1972) articulated the "wait-time" as an instructional construct. She found that quiet time following questions by a teacher and completed response by students resulted in positive behavior and attitudes by both parties. As a result, she urged teachers to wait a minimum of three seconds after a question and after a student responded to allow additional processing to occur. The most basic strategy teachers can adjust is their level of patience. It may require discipline, but learning to wait patiently in silence and in one position after asking questions will encourage positive outcomes for students. Demonstrating how to articulate a thought in uninterrupted silence will encourage students to patiently express themselves. Providing time to reflect on learning creates pathways to knowledge acquisition by building the natural desires to question or inquire (Short et al., 1996).

Learning to Learn Avocation

By design, Serious Comix does not adhere to traditional classroom conventions. Ideally, teacher and students form a community of individuals who convene to learn how the use of technology can enhance their literacy skills. I also see it as "learning to learn avocation." In this sense, in Serious Comix the accustomed preoccupation with the teacher teaching while the students learn takes a background position, and the positive emotions associated with learning based on personal interests move to the foreground. Participants must work to create a social atmosphere that is different from a traditional classroom. The question, then, is how teachers and students should jointly construct and manage the classroom community. How will they go about the process of learning to learn? The answer is straightforward: dialogue.

The Serious Comix instructional format uses dialogue to open the lines of communication for the students to collaborate, share, reflect, problem solve, and have an individualized learning experience. Opening the platform to enable students to have a voice and to be a partner in their own learning takes the focus off the act of learning. Students are able to refocus their energy on the act of being an accountable member in how they acquire and access information. Learning becomes part of them, and the act of learning takes a minor role. As they enjoy their newly created academic learning space, it becomes more joyful and almost like a hobby and a distraction from previous preoccupations. Such cultural interactions do not usually happen in a traditional classroom, where the primary focus is on teacher-led instruction. In Serious Comix, the learning practices of literacy and technology knowledge are conducted through the interactions between teacher and student, and between student and student.

Social Interaction and Collaboration

In order to develop a culture and a sense of community within a Serious Comix project, teachers must create a shared purpose, wherein each individual can develop a sense of identity that will bond him or her to the unit. Sewell's (1999) notion of *culture* (i.e., values and ways of acting and interacting that characterize a social group) includes attitudes and beliefs we have about learning and views we hold about schools and classrooms. Cultures are dynamic, complex, and changing; they include the ideations, symbols, behaviors, values, and beliefs shared by a group. In this respect, the culture of a Serious Comix project can resemble that of a school sports team or academic club. Students, as they learn from and interact with each other, gain insight into their individual similarities and differences and as a result acquire a shared sense of purpose.

As the teacher of a Serious Comix project, I do not correct a student's sitting positions or the level of his or her participation. This is not to say I allow students to disengage from the lessons. When I perceive that a student is not working I will, of course, prompt action. However, rather than telling the student to "get to work," I allow him or her to enact his or her own agency. That is, I acknowledge that a student sometimes needs time to gather his or her thoughts in order to begin working. As students are engaged in their creative activity, I remain present in the classroom. Walking around the room enables me to observe their sitting positions, writing postures, and individual ways of focusing, which could be misconstrued as not being engaged in work. For example, during one of the writing sessions, the students were asked to develop their story summaries into an outline. I observed the sitting positions of the students and the way they interacted with the material and noticed that although they looked very comfortable and relaxed, almost all the students were fully engaged in writing. I noticed that while the other students were engaged in the writing, Stewie was taking his time to mentally build up his thoughts. This was my opportunity to make myself available to him. However, rather than tell him to get busy, I inquired about his work in order to help him bring his ideas to the foreground. Shortly thereafter, Stewie could be seen in full writing mode.

The open dialogue format can be foreign to students and teachers alike. When students are in a mixed setting with a teacher-led discussion, I find that they prefer that questions be posed by the teacher, rather than by their peers. In this way, the formal classroom teacher-student/question-answer repartee can creep into a Serious Comix class. Effective use of the cogenerative dialogue format takes practice from all participants. But teachers who are committed to this learning strategy will find that even the most hesitant learners can overcome habits developed in the traditional classroom to keep the dialogue flowing.

Access to Technology, Instructor, Each Other

According to *Education Week's* annual Technology Counts survey (Bausell, 2008), the number of computers in public schools has increased steadily since 1998, leading to virtually no difference between poor schools and their wealthier counterparts. Likewise, the National Center for Education Statistics (in Parsad & Jones, 2005) reported that public schools in the United States have made progress in expanding Internet access, demonstrating an increase in Internet installation since 1996, when only about two-thirds of public schools had Internet access. Nearly 100% of public schools in the United States had access to the Internet, and no differences were observed based on school characteristics. In 2005, the ratio of students to instructional computers with Internet access in public schools was 3.8 to 1, a decrease from the 12.1 to 1 ratio first measured in 1998. Schools serving students living in poverty tend to use technology for more traditional memory-based and remedial activities, whereas schools serving wealthier communities are more likely to focus on communication and expression. In schools whose students are from higher-income families, 61% of teachers with computers use them in class compared to 50% of those teaching in schools with lower-income students (Lenhart, Rainie, & Lewis, 2001).

For a Serious Comix class to succeed, students must have access to technology hardware (including, for example, a printer, scanner, and interactive whiteboard) and software, but also to a knowledgeable and highly qualified teacher willing to effectively integrate these technologies into an open academic format. Marshall (2002) found evidence that the technology integrated by a qualified teacher "complements what a great teacher does naturally" and enhances students' learning experiences.

Differentiation of Instruction and One-to-One Coaching

Students learn, acquire, and retain information differently. Based on this fact, teachers must be equipped with a variety of instructional methods. Reaching a diversity of learners in this manner is known as differentiated instruction. According to Tomlinson (2001), differentiated instruction is a teaching theory based on varied instructional approaches that are readily adapted in relation to the learner. To differentiate instruction is to give students multiple options for receiving information and making sense of it. The teacher must recognize students' dissimilarities in background, culture, readiness, and language—factors that all affect the way a student learns.

In Serious Comix, differentiated instruction applies to the lesson content, the process or tools used, and the product from the students. It is very helpful for teachers to know their students' profiles in order to design specific teaching and learning objectives to accommodate each student's particular abilities and learning styles and to keep them engaged. Teachers also must use various materials, such as different levels and types of reading materials based on cultural interests, as well as various tools, from traditional pen and paper to different types of technology applications, to reach all learners.

Differentiated instruction also applies to student products. It is important to give students the flexibility to make decisions about how to individualize their products. This is higher-order thinking and a way to help students construct new knowledge and meaning from what they are learning.

When a teacher strives to provide differentiated instruction, lessons can be directed to a whole class while the relaxed and flexible design of the class culture permits one-to-one mini-instruction, as well as peer tutoring within the group.

Considering the Context of a Learning Environment

Students and educators are regulated by school policy and rules that are reinforced by classroom rules. The dialogue format I advocate for Serious Comix may, in some instances, be at odds with administration-sanctioned teaching methods—namely the traditional direct teaching method. Although some teachers in traditional settings include a dialogue format in their classrooms, students habituated to traditional teaching methods may be challenged when first experiencing a truly cogenerative class. They may not be accustomed to freely exploring their classroom and sharing without raising hands.

If a Serious Comix project is conducted within what is otherwise a direct teaching classroom, students may be confounded by the transition in teaching style. After all, we teach students to associate a given location with certain expectations—students tend to behave differently on a playground than, say, in the principal's office. For teachers who maintain a traditional direct teaching classroom, a Serious Comix project might be better conducted in a separate location: computer lab, flexible-use room, or someplace similar that allows for a safe but vigorous learning experience. As always, work with your administrative personnel for assistance, support, and guidance.

Classroom Layout

In a traditional classroom layout, the students' desks are usually set up for teacher-centered instruction. For example, in my school, classroom desks are set up in a in a grid pattern of three rows of four chairs. Students can see only the people to their left or right and the back of the head of the person in front. All students face the front, where the teacher, who is the focal point, stands.

With its dialogue format and focus on technology, the Serious Comix class requires reconsideration of the design of the physical classroom. The class requires a generous amount of space that allows for technology instruction and hands-on practice, face-to-face discussions among students, and desk space for students to complete graphic organizers and create illustrations.

It would be ideal to set up a space with two distinct areas. One area would facilitate instruction and discussion. In this area desks should be placed in a circular pattern that allows all students to see each other's facial expressions. The teacher would be among this cluster. This area should contain a focal point for instruction (e.g., an interactive whiteboard). The second area should contain individualized workstations for hands-on activities that still allow for discussions.

The Serious Comix students met in the computer lab, which was designated for the self-contained students once a week during lunch. The computer lab was split into two sections: half had 12 to 14 desk-chair combinations to facilitate discussions and simple instructions, and the other half had 12 to 14 individual computer terminals.

The technology hardware and programs available for Serious Comix were an interactive whiteboard, scanner and scanning application, and the Microsoft Office bundle, which includes Word and Power-Point. Arrangements were made to have the computer lab available for the student participants to use during their lunch and the last periods of the day to work on their comic books.

Encouraging Peer-to-Peer Dialogue

When I first initiated a discussion with my students about their comic books, I found that they were comfortable with questions from me but unsure about interacting with their peers using the open dialogue format. For example, Brock showed no hesitation in taking his turn to talk. He zeroed in on the focus of the discussion by clearly stating his story idea. However, when Stewie presented his idea, Brock, although he appeared to be very interested in what his peer had to say, at first directed his question about the topic to the teacher, me, instead of Stewie. This showed me that Brock would need a little modeling and encouragement from me. Stewie was comfortable answering my questions, but when Brock showed interest by asking him a question, his behavior turned shy.

Teacher	Brock, what book do you think you want to create?
Brock	Ninja.
Teacher	A Ninja book? Okay, what about the ninjas, what do you think they will do?
Brock	Battle for world peace.
Teacher	Battle for world peace. That is a good topic.
Brock	In Tokyo.
Teacher	In Tokyo, why not New York?
Brock	'Cause ninjas are not in New York. They belong in Tokyo, Japan, or in China.
Teacher	Stewie, what do you think you would like to do?
Stewie	*(Speaking too softly for everyone to hear)* I think a kid that gets sucked into TV.
Teacher	Say it one more time. I didn't quite hear you.
Stewie	A kid that goes into the TV world.
Teacher	Oh, okay fantasy. That is interesting. What would he do in the TV? What would he do there?

> **Brock**   *(Directing his question to the teacher)* Does he mean like, surfing through the channels?
>
> **Teacher**   *(Encouraging open dialogue)* You could ask him.
>
> **Brock**   Will he surf through the channels?
>
> **Stewie**   *(Laughs and puts his head down. Brock also laughs and puts his head down.)*

Although this might not seem like a big advancement, it is small steps like these that build a classroom where students can learn from each other as well as from the teacher.

When students are involved in a learning community that collectively values peer learning and improved technology knowledge and skills, these students can become energized to produce a new culture that is in their best interest, long term. Indeed, a Serious Comix project can be a catalyst for students to begin identifying themselves as technology users and peer tutors (we will explore this idea in depth in Chapter 3). This positive culture can be replicated in other places for the benefit of all students.

STUDENT OWNERSHIP OF LEARNING

B ased on my experience, most students seem comfortable using technology. When using technology, kids don't seem to fear looking silly or odd, or not understanding how something works—they just keep trying until they figure it out. In my school, many students walk around with devices such as mobile phones and handheld video games. However, I have found that these students are often not adept at transferring the technology skills learned by using their personal devices to academic learning, and they may not even be aware that there is a connection. This observation—that when students learn to use technology only in ways not related to academic function, they appear less capable of transferring these skills to the academic arena—is supported by Wenger (1999). These students have the dexterity and basic knowledge needed to use technology, but seem unmotivated or lost when asked to apply these skills toward academic work.

In my view, the problem for students isn't that the technology is difficult to use or even that the academic material itself is too difficult or uninteresting. The problem is that students feel no sense of ownership in their academic work. Without that sense of ownership, they seem to be less able (or willing) to transfer knowledge or skills. The question, then, is how to help students achieve ownership of their learning.

Triggering the Skills Transfer

The essential reason I employed the cogenerative dialogue format in the Serious Comix project was to create a learning community that facilitates ownership of learning. As a teacher with technology knowledge and skill, I intended my practices to expand the students' capacity to collaborate with and learn from each other. Through the agency afforded in the computer lab, students labeled as emotionally disturbed felt a coresponsibility for our Serious Comix project that, in time, transformed into a desire to help their fellow students use technology to learn. All these students gained new visions for technology use within the classroom and at home.

A New Classroom Culture

Student involvement in the teaching of peers can be a somewhat uncomfortable shift for teachers. In a Serious Comix classroom, the teacher is allowed, even encouraged, to move past the pervasive teacher-centered view of education. Doing so allows the students and the teacher, as a community of learners, to benefit from the range of individual expertise that is contained within the entire group.

Collins (2004) believes that high levels of focused, positive emotional energy create a kind of collective effervescence, which can have long-term consequences for interaction rituals that, in turn, can be carried over after the individual has left the situation. In other words, if students feel energized about their new technology skills and writing progress, they will be more likely to put their newly acquired capital to work in their classroom, school work, and home. Peer tutoring is integral to creating such a positive environment.

Peer Tutoring

The practice of cogenerative dialogue does not absolve teachers from the basics of good instruction. Teachers, of course, must model the appropriate use of classroom technologies and demonstrate to students how these technologies apply to the project. To accomplish this, instruction should connect specific technologies together using a sensibility that itself is interactive. For example, modeling the use of graphic organizers should highlight the skills and concepts students need to effectively use the Windows environment, which means, in turn, that the Windows environment should be broken down into teachable and learnable parts as related to effective use of the graphic organizer. Periodic assessments of learning should be made through asking questions of the students and encouraging students to ask questions of the teacher and each other.

However good the instruction is, and even though all participants are introduced to the functions of a software application at the same time, not all students will be able to comprehend at the same level. Roughly speaking, students will fall into one of two groups of learners—confident or struggling. Confident students can be thought of as performing above the group level. These are students whose interest in technology may be such that they can acquire new technology skills with minimal guidance. These students are the best candidates for becoming peer tutors. Struggling students are those who, at times, seem lost and often require additional coaching. A tech-focused classroom with continued exposure to new technology might seem a daunting place for these students. But in the Serious Comix classroom, where open dialogue is coupled with a social setting that embraces peer teaching, these struggling students are offered a way to achieve meaningful success.

Peer tutoring can facilitate mutual respect and synchrony that builds strong levels of solidarity. Immediately after the teacher-led instruction, a peer tutor might be able to take his or her newly acquired information and redirect it in a linear manner for a peer learner. The peer tutor might set the tone for a mini-session by engaging the focus of another student by asking questions and modeling different functions. In turn, the learner's attention and responses might indicate appreciation, resulting in positive rein-forcement of the peer tutor's efforts. Indeed, a peer tutor's alertness might coexist with his or her "student's" attention and focus on every word, gesture, and motion.

A peer tutor's unsolicited assistance to his or her peers is worthy of teacher praise. This offer and acceptance of assistance is a sign of mutual respect between students. Peer tutoring can also help teachers reduce apprehensions they may have about their own abilities, the use of multiple technology applications, and the cogenerative dialogue class structure itself. Peer tutoring interactions also reveal learning possibilities for the student receiving instruction; no longer is the teacher seen as the sole resource for acquiring new skills.

In the following example, Brock helped KK with scanning. Close analysis shows Brock's teaching ability as well as the time and consideration he takes to ensure that KK understands each step.

Brock: First you put the paper face down. The paper should be at the top right corner.

Shut it.

I don't know if it resets or something, so you might want to press the green start button.

Then this will be there, the pop-up window of the directory.

To improve your coloring, you choose either pure black and white or color.

Then you press Preview.

To preview how good it comes out. If the preview is good you then scan it.

First, you change the name.

Okay, then you press Browse to see what folder . . . My folder "Brock." We already have the folder open. And, press Save to start scanning.

And that's all there is to scanning.

KK: So, that's it, right there in the folder?

Brock: You tell me, where is it?

Positive Environment

The computer lab in my school was equipped with outdated Apple and Dell desktop computers, and at any given time two or three computers were not working. The old hardware had a real impact on student learning. These computers were very slow to start up, had difficulty running multiple programs, and often spontaneously shut down because of overheating. The software on the computers was comparably outdated, with Microsoft Office 2003 or 2004 applications. These issues were sources of irritation for students and teachers alike.

Once Serious Comix students were in the groove of working on their comic books, they became aware of the slowness of this outdated technology. They sometimes had trouble even opening applications and processing work. Although this is a burden for any user, it was an especially heavy one for these novice users who had not yet become accustomed to constantly saving their work.

During one session, as Brock was typing in Word, his PC shut down. He became angry and banged on the table. He was sure he had lost his work. Of course I had repeated the necessary instruction to "save your work" many times previously, but it was during this particular incident that this message finally registered with Brock. Once his machine was back up and running, he opened Word and discovered that his work had been saved. He was relieved. More importantly, following this experience, Brock would periodically call out to the others, "Everyone, remember always save your work so if you have to restart the most recent work will be there."

The other students began to build solidarity from Brock's words—they had found a way to overcome the persistent hardware limitations they endured. This, in turn, created positive emotional energy: saving their work reduced their anxiety and built patience with the old equipment. Soon the Serious Comix members were constantly reminding one another, "Don't forget to save your work!" This newly acquired knowledge became a rule for working with the old equipment.

Ultimately, if students feel successful doing activities they enjoy (in this case, creating digital storyboards), this intrinsic feeling of enjoyment might spill over into other academic areas. The Serious Comix project is designed to encourage students to enjoy a life of learning.

Chapter 4

CREATING SERIOUS COMIX: FOUNDATIONS

To create a Serious Comix digital storyboard, students engage in a combination of writing, word processing, illustration creation, and scanning. Then they bring the material together into a comic-strip–style format within a presentation program. The details of the lessons can be found in the Lesson Plans section. In this chapter, I discuss some foundational activities and skills that will help make the project go smoothly.

Students find the comic book format easy to understand and use. Creating illustrations helps students with creating text and the limited text in each frame is less intimidating to those for whom writing is a challenge. The clearly defined framing and sequencing of a comic helps students better understand the critical literary points of a story and incorporate them into their own comics. Because comic books are laid out in frames, it is easy for student authors to easily jump ahead and go back as necessary during the creative process, adding and removing material as necessary.

Foundations for Building Literacy

Prewriting Activity

As a prewriting activity, in the first session the instructor should facilitate a class dialogue that starts the students talking about their ideas, opinions, and feelings about comics and the stories they want to tell. The purpose of this discussion is to help students select a story topic. Instructors should engage students through questions that enable them to recall prior knowledge about the important elements of a story, including title, main idea, characters, setting, mood, and problems. Students should also be reminded of how the main idea of a story must be carried through the three essential parts of a story: the beginning, middle, and conclusion. For the Serious Comix project, the beginning of a student-created comic should introduce the theme and issues of the story; the middle should focus on the characters and problems; and the conclusion should detail how the problems are resolved.

Teachers will likely find that during the prewriting discussion, students will bring up stories about their weekends, cartoons they saw recently, or the plot of their favorite comic book or series. This open discussion allows students to encounter and consider stories and characters brought up by others that may differ from their own ideas and experiences.

It may be helpful to provide examples of student- or commercially created comics during this discussion. However, keep in mind that students may latch onto these examples for inspiration, so to discourage copying, instructors should introduce them in a way that discourages students from shortcutting the creative process.

Graphic Organizers and the Writing Process

In a Serious Comix project, students demonstrate their progress in literacy learning as they organize ideas into stories, visualize a format and design for their stories, and develop problem-solving skills during the revision process to select the most essential information and discover satisfying endings to their stories. Using graphic organizers in this writing process helps students learn how to think visually and then effectively express those thoughts.

These visual learning aids are designed to help students represent knowledge, concepts, and ideas in an organized manner. Students are able to visually see clues that map out a theme and storyline.

A variety of organizers are available for story development (series of event chain, descriptive, thematic map, network tree); teachers must recognize which organizer is best for their particular students. Regardless of the graphic organizers chosen, the observed benefits of using such a tool are student improvement in vocabulary skills (Moore & Readence, 1984) and comprehension (Boyle & Weishaar, 1997). These improvements are applicable to all subjects. Furthermore, Boyle and Weishaar (1997) reported successful learning outcomes for students with learning disabilities. I can report that my Serious Comix students experienced this sort of success, as well. Marzano (in Marzano, Pickering, & Pollock, 2001) also notes the advantages of graphic organizers:

> Graphic organizers are perhaps the most common way to help students generate nonlinguistic representations. . . . Graphic organizers combine the linguistic mode in that they use words and phrases, and the nonlinguistic mode in that they use symbols and arrows to represents relationships. (p. 75)

Graphic organizers are an excellent scaffolding tool, allowing visual learners, struggling writers, and English language learners to rely on visual symbols to differentiate and show relationships between story elements. Using graphic organizers helps students to make connections between what they write and what they draw. Graphic organizers also help the students maintain focus, identify relationships among their ideas, and enhance their recall skills through referencing their own created material.

Two types of graphic organizers were used in the Serious Comix class to help students create their comics: a graphic organizer for story writing that aids students in capturing story elements, and a graphic organizer for comic book creation (blank comic panels) that aids in bringing the writing and illustrations together into a logical storyline. Figures 4.1 and 4.2 show examples of two types of graphic organizers that can be used in this project.

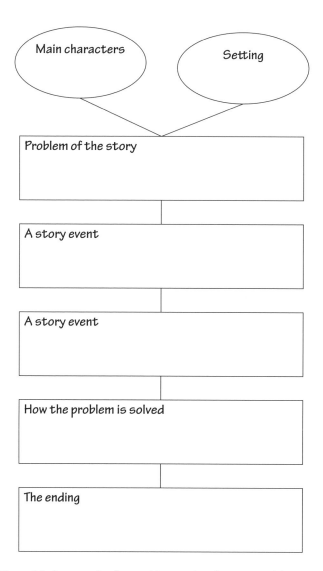

Figure 4.1 An example of a graphic organizer for story writing

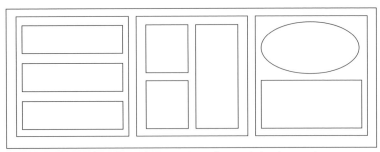

Figure 4.2 Examples of graphic organizers for comic book creation

If you do not already have a story outline map that you like to use, I encourage you to design one yourself or search the Internet to find one that would work best for your project and students. As I went about the process of designing the graphic organizers for my Serious Comix project, I considered many factors. I wanted them to be easy for students to use. I also wanted the organizers to help students clarify ideas, enhance reading comprehension, and promote writing skills. I believe that the graphic organizers I created met these expectations, and I am certain that without them the Serious Comix experience would have been less successful.

Graphic Organizer for Story Writing

The graphic organizer for story writing helps students brainstorm, plot, and draft their stories based on the question, "What are some things that a story needs?" This graphic organizer helps enable students to access their prior knowledge by visually representing story elements. It also helps students remember all the important parts of a story when writing. The layout of the map should be flexible and easy to use. As the project progresses, students should be able to question themselves and each other about the type of story they are creating. Although not all students experience difficulty in writing without visual aids, many do, and this organizer will help all students write a logical story by following a sequence of ideas and the basics of storytelling conventions. Even the most challenged student will be able to tell a story in a succinct, unfolding manner.

Graphic Organizer for Comic Book Creation

The graphic organizer for comic book creation helps students unite their story and their images in an organized manner before they attempt to digitize the project. This organizer should consist of simple blank comic book panels; students will decide which words and which illustration will fill each panel. You as the instructor may choose to limit the number of panels per story, or you might choose to allow the length of the story and number of finished illustrations to dictate the number of panels.

Because students are not required to write a certain number of words or sentences, the comic book panel will likely feel manageable and friendly to them. The images students create support their attempts to express their ideas with written language. A student's images convey the meaning of his or her story—and a student who has expressed a story visually can often more easily transfer that story into text. In this way, students are engaged in their own literacy learning. In addition, teachers can use each student's graphic organizers to readily assess the student's progress and learning.

Foundations for Technology Learning

In terms of technology literacy, the educator must decide what sort of skills to emphasize. This determination has many components, such as student readiness, teacher readiness, availability of technology, and curriculum demands. There is no one right way to integrate technology.

Teachers will need to focus student use of these technologies in terms of creating and presenting a digital storyboard. If the teacher directs students to use pencils and paper to create storyboards, then in a later step students will need to transfer their images and handwritten work into a digital format.

Selecting Technology Tools

The technology tools available in most computer labs should be sufficient to conduct a Serious Comix class: an interactive whiteboard, a computer with word processing and presentation software for each student, and a scanner.

In my class I used personal computers with a Windows operating system and a Microsoft Office software bundle that included Word and PowerPoint. However, there are other sources for these tools, such as OpenOffice (OpenOffice.org), which is a free, open-source office productivity software suite that includes word processing, spreadsheets, presentations, graphics, and databases. The main thing is to use basic digital technologies that students are likely to encounter in other settings such as other classes, at home, or in a workplace.

By no means is this an exhaustive list of technologies that could be used to conduct a Serious Comix project. Innovative, tech-forward teachers may choose to use software that is designed specifically to create comics or animations. Presentations of the finished comics may take place online in a public space such as YouTube or on a school's private intranet. The flexibility and mutability of digital technology allows for innumerable variations.

However, although digital technology is ever changing, a few important considerations do not change. In an educational setting, all computers, networks, software applications, and so on are the property of the school. Teachers must seek approval before downloading applications onto school systems. Also, because many schools and teachers cannot afford expensive retail software and licenses, budgetary realities may preclude upgrades. Teachers may be forced to use worn-out hardware and outdated software. It is no surprise, then, that professional educators have long relied on freeware and shareware to keep current with advances in digital technologies.

Freeware is computer software that is licensed for use at no cost. It is either fully functional for an unlimited time or has only basic functions enabled with a fully functional version available commercially or as shareware. Shareware is software that is available to users on a trial basis or trial version (limited features or full version for a period of time) and that requires payment (a nominal fee) at the end of the trial period for continued access and use. Once the software license is purchased, the software's functionality and support will be extended.

Introducing Technology Tools Using an Interactive Whiteboard

The interactive whiteboard is useful to a Serious Comix project because the instructor can use it to demonstrate each application, model lesson objectives, and then allow students to use it to practice their public speaking skills and ultimately present their completed projects to a larger class. In evaluating the usage of the interactive whiteboard in elementary schools with students labeled with disabilities, researchers have found that students listen, hear, and are visually engaged in learning (Sani, 2007). According to Ngao (2006), the interactive whiteboard enhances teaching, particularly with students with disabilities.

The basic functionality of an interactive whiteboard is a touch screen that allows the user access to different environments. The interactive whiteboard is connected to a computer and projector. The computer's desktop is displayed via the projector onto the board's surface. The user is able to manipulate the function tools with the pens and other input devices.

When instructing students, I am easily able to bring up the Windows desktop environment on the whiteboard. Using language that is easy to follow, I highlight the interactive capabilities of the desktop or graphical user interface (GUI) and describe the elements found on the desktop, such as icons, windows, toolbars, folders, and wallpapers. And, by using the terminology found on the screen, I ensure that the participants make the connection between each step.

When introducing a new concept, such as the use of an interactive whiteboard, I explain to students the similarities between using this new tool and a tool they may already be familiar with—say, a Windows computer. In addition to providing general instruction at the interactive whiteboard, I explain the use of certain hardware items that are connected to the interactive whiteboard. I tell them that this equipment is the same as the computers located at their individual workstations. The steps I demonstrate at the interactive whiteboard are the same steps that students use on their individual computers. Thus, as students learn to perform such tasks as finding the shared drive, creating a personal folder to store work, and functioning within the Windows environment, they are also learning the tools of the interactive whiteboard—itself a key component of a dialogue-based classroom.

The use of an interactive whiteboard can also allow students to demonstrate the extent to which they can work with different technologies and applications. In a setting that employs dialogue, students who are confident with these technologies will likely be more than willing to show their individual works in progress and demonstrate their understanding of both the applications and the interactive whiteboard touch directives. Less accomplished technology users will often be interested in learning from their peer tutors. A peer tutor might, for example, engage in a mini-presentation to tell his or her story-in-progress and showcase any newly acquired technology skills (as we saw in Chapter 3).

The teacher can model this sort of mini-presentation. It may be helpful to emphasize the importance of understanding the functions of the software in creating and assembling a digital storyboard. Emphasis could also be placed on discussing writing-process issues, the help that peer review can provide, the importance of writing down information and directions, and the advantages of using class time efficiently and effectively.

Image Scanner

The image scanner is an input device that enables individuals to optically scan images and printed or handwritten text to a digital file. In Serious Comix, students who have access to an image scanner can draw on a paper graphic organizer and then import the digital version of that work into a digital storyboard. The digital result can be an accurate, high-quality reproduction of the students' hand-drawn comic strip panels. Just as importantly in terms of technology literacy, students are able to capture, retrieve, store, and edit their digital images. These are skills that have value far beyond the Serious Comix project.

A scanner provides flexibility for students who may not have the ability or technical skill needed to create images solely using computer software. A teacher's knowledge of this technology and thorough interactive modeling enable students to quickly acquire the skills they need to complete the Serious Comix project. As their knowledge of technology, literacy, and presentation skills grow, confident students become central figures in a cogenerative dialogue classroom. This sort of independence enables these students to be less dependent on the teacher and more willing to assume the role of a peer teacher.

Although no two scanners are exactly alike, all perform the same essential functions for use in Serious Comix. Students must work with both the scanner hardware and the scanner application software to transfer their hand-drawn art into a digital format.

One Serious Comix class session should be dedicated to introducing scanning—its functions and terminology. A good formula for presenting new technology, either a software application or hardware, is to engage students by directly interacting with the device.

The sensibilities a teacher uses to demonstrate word processing (Word), presentation (PowerPoint), and interactive whiteboard software should be used to demonstrate whatever software a given scanner uses. Particular emphasis should be placed on similarities in terms of task management, such as opening an application and creating, saving, and locating files.

The utilities specific to the scanning software must be modeled as well. Students must also practice using software that allows them to alter the resolution of an image, add metadata (information about an image), and more.

Software Applications

An interactive instructional approach for working with software applications is a must. In other words, teachers must emphasize the similarities among applications. This emphasis allows students to effectively coordinate their learning activities. In the case of Microsoft applications, for example, teachers should emphasize the similarities in locating, opening, saving, and closing files. This emphasis helps students understand the similarities of task steps, no matter if they are using Word or PowerPoint, a desktop computer or an interactive whiteboard. This focus on similarities is a meaningful way to help make technology transparent to students. Students can focus their efforts on making meaningful content (comics) instead of obsessing about the differences between drop-down menus. Moreover, students can transfer common best-use strategies to software applications from other software makers.

The Microsoft Office Environment

The Microsoft Office environment is a suite of interrelated desktop applications that includes word processing software (Word) and presentation software (PowerPoint). It is no coincidence that Word and PowerPoint are used in Serious Comix. According to Forrester

2009 research, some version of Microsoft Office is used in 80% of enterprises. In all likelihood, students will encounter this particular software brand beyond the classroom, and so they should have some practice using it. In addition, Microsoft applications share many of the same features, including toolbars, menu bars, and scroll bars. This design sensibility helps make this software transparent to users. Practically speaking, during week 1, teachers should use the interactive whiteboard to model the use of the Microsoft Office environment. Then, at the beginning of week 2, class time can be dedicated to direct instruction in Word.

In Serious Comix, students are asked to use Word to create story summaries. These summaries are based on the work students capture on their graphic organizers. The instruction for using Word emphasizes basic functions: creating and naming file folders, opening the application, typing text, running a spell check, and saving work to file folders.

Writing is often a very difficult task for students, yet even the most intimidated can learn to be more confident in attempting it. Rewriting and revising are particularly challenging for students who are learning how to communicate their ideas effectively. Peck and Dorricott (1994) reported that when students use the function tools of word processing software (editing, formatting, spelling, and grammar checker), they are less frustrated, because revision time is reduced. Basic word processing skills also enable students to create summaries in a more organized manner.

In a Serious Comix setting, the ease of use and functions of a word processing application lead to an effective teaching and learning environment. Typing and revising text, changing the font, formatting text, using the spell checker, and producing clean and readable text gives students a full sense of authorship. Students show more willingness to make changes to their digital text than to handwritten work, in large part because word processing software eliminates the tedious tasks related to reworking handwritten drafts. Instead, students can spend more time on developing the story content and images in their digital comic books. This, in turn, increases opportunities for peer-to-peer collaboration.

Publishing for Presentation

Completing a Serious Comix project requires that students revise and edit, and then present their finished product to the members of class. In the revision stage, students review the images they created and revise their stories. (Some students generate text after creating illustrations, whereas others write text and then create images.) These revisions include adding background color, layout refinements, transitions, image colors, callouts, and any other feature students deems necessary to enhance their digital comic. Before presentation, students can add supplemental materials such as character biographies and copyright information. In addition to reading their stories during a class presentation, students should be encouraged to articulate reasons behind their choices.

PowerPoint is a flexible application with many potential uses. Teachers should focus student learning on its usability in terms of creating interactive text, animations, and sound effects and inserting graphics. Students already familiar with Microsoft Word should be able to perform basic functions in PowerPoint such as locating, starting, saving, and closing files. To help students recognize the sorts of presentations they can make using PowerPoint, teachers can animate their software demonstration. The effect can be highly engaging—interactive lessons that highlight key features of the software, use proper terminology, and provide concrete examples for student-created storyboards.

The use of PowerPoint as a presentation program provides an effective approach to both interactive instruction and student work. When students can actually see the functions of the presentation program in conjunction with a teacher demonstration that models them, students are empowered to confidently display their digital storyboards.

PowerPoint allows students to easily and quickly create slides using the content from their graphic organizers. The slide stack metaphor helps students to transfer content from graphic organizers to the digital format and then efficiently make revisions. These revision skills extend beyond the application itself.

If you don't have access to PowerPoint, Google offers a similar service, free of charge, called Google Slides (http://support.google.com/drive/bin/answer.py?hl=en&answer=1685857).

Chapter 5

REFLECTIONS

I find that the great thing in this world is not so much
where we stand, as in what direction we are moving.

—Oliver Wendell Holmes

At the close of my Serious Comix project, I returned the
students to their respective classrooms. As I said my good-byes
to Brock, Stewie, KK, and the others, I realized that I had forgotten
my folders and journal in the computer lab. When I entered the
lab, Mr. O., the school's computer teacher, offered some unsolicited
comments about the Serious Comix project and, in particular, the
cogenerative dialogue activities he had observed.

Mr. O. expressed amazement at the students' ability to learn many
different technology applications, their manner of communication
with each other, and their level of productivity. He went on to say
that "their disabilities could have created a very different environment." He spoke from the perspective of a special education teacher
who worked with emotionally disturbed students—Mr. O. had
learned to anticipate disruptions. When he did not see the Serious
Comix students create disruptions, it renewed his hope for students
labeled with disabilities. In fact, he had noticed that Stewie and
Brock had made regular visits to the computer lab to work on their
projects and to discuss how to help each other.

Mr. O. commented on the students' high level of commitment to
learning different technologies and their ability to focus on the end
results. He mentioned how their dispositions changed as a result of
being members of the Serious Comix project. Mr. O. was particularly impressed that Brock and Stewie emerged as peer tutors. In
the beginning, both boys were shy, awkward using technology, and

easily frustrated with the slow and outdated computers. Moreover, the cogenerative dialogue format was new to them. As time passed, the students became more and more confident as their technology knowledge and skills increased and their projects took shape.

As I thought about how Mr. O. had expected that there might be disruptions from these students, I admitted to myself that I, too, had had similar concerns. As a teacher who works in a special education setting, I was well aware of the sudden and spontaneous outbursts that can occur. In my six years of teaching, I have worked with self-contained students classified as emotionally disturbed. I have witnessed students' aggressive behaviors, such as bullying, physical altercations, and the destruction of property.

After the end of the Serious Comix project, I asked Brock and Stewie's teachers if they had noticed any academic or behavioral changes in them. The teachers reported that both Stewie and Brock were more engaged in class participation and group activities—as one teacher put it, "considerably more acceptable behaviors." Brock and Stewie had taken a greater interest in reading different types of academic materials; I was told that they both made regular visits to the in-school library to check out books. At the end of school year, Brock and Stewie's English language arts (ELA) scores increased one full level, from 2 to 3. (In the New York City school system, test scores are indicated by four levels, 1 being the lowest, and 4 the highest.) I cannot say for sure that the changes are a result of being in the Serious Comix project; however, I am certain that their experiences in that learning environment had a strong, positive impact on them.

Brock and Stewie are two amazing boys who demonstrated great academic abilities through the use of technology. In Serious Comix, they initiated dialogue, demonstrated various technological functions and activities on the interactive whiteboard, and offered assistance to their peers.

I believe in giving students the freedom to express their culture, speech, learning styles, and, by way of Serious Comix, teaching abilities. This project can help teachers to move past labels and see students as individuals capable of mastering technology and literacy knowledge and skills. Technology and literacy must become part of every student's life, in and out of school.

In Serioux Comix, we were individuals who became a group. In the process, we let our desire to learn from each other and our shared experiences lead us. I walked away from the group a renewed person and a better teacher and researcher. In the beginning, I thought only about offering something brilliant to these students. But as we worked together, they gave me back something more than words can express. I hope you will consider my experiences and create a Serious Comix project of your own!

SERIOUS COMIX LESSON PLANS

Serious Comix Lesson Plans Overview

My Serious Comix project was divided into six classroom sessions. Because the students and I met only once a week (50 minutes per session) over six weeks, it was imperative that the students practice independently to develop their skills.

These sessions could be integrated into subject areas to extend the time and to accommodate a larger class of students. Once students internalize the value of learning, they often begin to work independently outside of the class.

The following is an overview of the lesson plans.

Setup

> *Title:* Serious Comix
>
> *Grade Level:* 3–12 (Ages 8–18)
>
> *Subject Areas:* English language arts, visual arts, instructional technology
>
> *Duration:* Six 45- to 90-minute lessons
>
> *Location:* Computer lab or similarly equipped classroom; student access to the location outside of class time for practice and development is necessary

Teaching Goals

- Help students develop reading and writing skills through the use of graphic organizers

- Help students develop reading and writing skills and improve visual literacy through creation and/or use of illustrations and text together to tell a story

- Introduce students to basic word processing and presentation software via modeling; promote skill development through hands-on practice

- Employ conversational instruction with open-ended questions delivered through discussion format (cogenerative dialogue)

- Enable and encourage peer interaction and coaching

Student Learning Goals

- Improve reading, writing, and visual literacy through the creation of digital storyboards

- Meet curriculum requirements in English language arts (ELA) in reading, writing, and presentation

- Improve technology literacy

Equipment and Materials

Hardware: personal computers, interactive whiteboard, scanner

Software: Microsoft Word and PowerPoint; or similar word processing and presentation software. Graphics software is suggested but not required.

Graphic Organizers: Two types of graphic organizers are needed, one for story writing and one for story creation. A simple Internet search on the words "graphic organizer for story writing" will yield a plethora of ready-made graphic organizers, for any age range, that will work for this project. Choose a graphic organizer that covers the major elements of story writing such as characters, setting, plot, climax, and conclusion. Many graphic organizers of this type also answer the questions *who, what, where, when, why,* and *how.*

Also search for a graphic organizer specifically designed for comic book creation, with blank comic book panels. This will help students plan out each individual panel in their comic book.

Art Materials: paper, pencils, colored pencils, pens, and markers, and crayons (art created this way will be scanned to digital format. Alternatively, students could create their art digitally from the start using a graphics program; or, with instructor support, they could seek out and use existing copyright-free art as illustrations.)

Additional Material: sample comic books for inspiration

Lesson Plans

The Serious Comix program is based on a six-lesson schedule, listed below. The instructor should strive to have the flexibility to accommodate individual student learning by way of one-to-one tutoring, peer coaching, and full-class instruction.

The *On Their Own* sections provide guidance for work to be done outside of class.

> *Lesson 1:* Introduction to Comic Books, Technology Tools, and Cogenerative Dialogue
> > *On Their Own:* Tech Tool Practice
>
> *Lesson 2:* Story Writing and Illustration Creation Using Graphic Organizers, Part I
> > *On Their Own:* Writing and Illustrating
>
> *Lesson 3:* Story Writing and Illustration Creation Using Graphic Organizers, Part II
> > *On Their Own:* Tech Tool Practice, Storyboard Creation
>
> *Lesson 4:* Scanning Illustrations to Digital Format
> > *On Their Own:* Tech Tool Practice
>
> *Lesson 5:* Creating Digital Comic Books in PowerPoint
> > *On Their Own:* Tech Tool Practice, Presentation Practice
>
> *Lesson 6:* Presenting Digital Comic Book to Peers

Introduction to Comic Books, Technology Tools, and Cogenerative Dialogue

During this first lesson, the instructor outlines the Serious Comix project for students. Students are introduced to the essentials of story writing for comic books, as well as the basic functionality of the interactive whiteboard and Windows environments. Students are also introduced to the cogenerative dialogue format of the class.

Objectives

Teaching

The instructor will:

- Introduce and discuss the open dialogue format of the class

- Present an overview of rules, including how students should respect each other and technology

- Depending on grade level, introduce or review the parts of a story (e.g., characters, setting, plot, climax, and conclusion)

- Hand out and explain the graphic organizer for story writing

- Introduce students to the Microsoft Office environment and the interactive whiteboard

Learning

Students should understand:

- The open dialogue format of the class and the rules regarding participation

- The parts of a story

- How the graphic organizer will help them write a story

- How to navigate the Microsoft Office environment and use the interactive whiteboard

Lesson Description

Open the lesson with a discussion of the open dialogue format. Explain that the class will be run differently than most of their classes and that you hope they will enjoy and benefit from the additional freedom of this new format. Also explain expectations for behavior and consequences for misbehavior.

Next, start a group discussion of comic books and the comic book format (comic strips work for discussion as well). What makes comic books different from other literature? How do the words and images work together to tell a story? What are some comic book conventions, such as typographic and illustrative ways of conveying happiness, sadness, fear, or action?

Depending on the age of your students, introduce or review the parts of a story, including characters, setting, plot, climax, and conclusion. Explain that students will be using graphic organizers to help create their comic books, and hand out the graphic organizer for story writing.

Finally, using the interactive whiteboard, introduce or review the Microsoft Office environment, including basic navigation in Word and PowerPoint. Emphasize similarities between the programs. Discuss how and where students should save their work, and how they should name files.

On Their Own

Tech Tool Practice: Students should practice navigating the Microsoft Office environment, including Word and Power-Point. Consider having them create a Word document, populate it with story ideas, name the file correctly, and save it to the correct directory. Encourage students to coach each other on proper technology use. Remind students to save their work often.

Story Writing and Illustration Creation Using Graphic Organizers, Part I

During the second lesson, students will discuss story ideas with each other and begin to draft their stories using their graphic organizers. At the same time, students will create illustrations to fit their story ideas. Students will consider how the words and the text work together to tell a story.

Objectives

Teaching

The instructor will:

- Remind students about the open dialogue format of the class

- Review the parts of a story and the use of the graphic organizer for story writing

- Facilitate an open discussion among students about their story ideas

- Help students begin to capture story elements on their graphic organizers for story writing

- Help students understand how story elements and illustrations inform each other

Learning

Students should understand:

- The parts of a story

- The inspirational value of peer discussion and feedback

- How to use the graphic organizer for story writing to capture their story ideas

- How story elements and illustrations inform each other

Lesson Description

Open the lesson with a review of the open dialogue format. Also review the parts of a story and how to use the graphic organizer for story writing. To model use of this graphic organizer, consider having the group help you populate a blank graphic organizer with story elements from a well-known fairy tale.

Next, facilitate an open discussion among students about their story ideas. Students will likely depend on the teacher at first to sustain the discussion; encourage them to address each other directly and respectfully.

Finally, students should begin to capture story elements on their graphic organizers. Some students will prefer to write and then illustrate; others may prefer to create illustrations and then write. Attempt to balance each student's individual working time with time for discussion and feedback from peers. Students should understand that story creation is an iterative process. Help students make connections between the words they write and the illustrations they create.

Depending on the technology available, you may choose to have students handwrite and hand-draw; or students could type stories into a digital graphic organizer and create illustrations in a graphic design program. Another option is to have students search for copyright-free illustrations rather than creating their own. If illustrating by hand, students should create each illustration on a separate piece of paper, because they will be scanning their illustrations to digital format in a future lesson. If students are creating art digitally, each illustration should be created in a separate file.

On Their Own

Writing and Illustrating: Students should continue to capture their story ideas and create illustrations.

Story Writing and Illustration Creation Using Graphic Organizers, Part II

During the third lesson, students will continue refining their stories and illustrations with input from their peers, with the objective of getting their graphic organizers completely filled in, finishing their stories, and completing their illustrations. Students will type their stories into a word processing program, use the spell-check and grammar functions, and name and save the document. Students will be introduced to the graphic organizer for comic book creation.

Objectives

Teaching

The instructor will:

- Review how to navigate the Microsoft Office environment and use the interactive whiteboard

- Help students finish capturing story elements on their graphic organizers for story writing

- Have students save their stories as Word documents

- Hand out the graphic organizer for comic book creation and explain its use

Learning

Students should understand:

- How story elements and illustrations inform each other

- How to navigate the Microsoft Office environment and Word

- How to use the graphic organizer for comic book creation

Lesson Description

Lead a quick review of the Microsoft Office environment and Word, including using the spell-check and grammar-check functions, and how to name files and where to save them.

Encourage students to complete their graphic organizers for story creation and use the captured elements to write their stories. Have students type their stories in Word, use the spell-check and grammar-check functions, and name and save the files according to your instructions. Remind students to save their work often. Students should also finish their illustrations.

Hand out the graphic organizer for comic book creation. Explain that students will need to begin deciding which text and which illustration will be assigned to each panel to create a storyboard. The instructor should decide ahead of time whether the number of panels for student comic books will be limited, or whether students may use as many panels as they need.

On Their Own

Tech Tool Practice: If students are unable to finish capturing their stories as a word processing document during class time, they should complete this activity outside class.

Storyboard Creation: Using their graphic organizer for comic book creation, students should continue assigning text and illustrations to each panel.

Scanning Illustrations to Digital Format

During the fourth lesson, students will learn how to scan their illustrations to create digital files. More advanced students will be encouraged to coach their peers on use of the scanner. Students will be completing their storyboards as they wait their turn to use the scanner.

Objectives

Teaching

The instructor will:

- Demonstrate the use of the scanner and scanning software

- Explain how to best name and save digital illustrations in an organized manner for future use

- Encourage students who understand scanning well to coach their peers

- Help students finish their storyboards, using the graphic organizer for comic book creation

Learning

Students should understand:

- How to use the scanner and scanning software

- The importance of naming and organizing their digital illustrations appropriately

- How to use the graphic organizer for comic book creation to complete their storyboards

Lesson Description

Teach students how to use the scanner and scanning software, and how to name files and where to save them. It is important that students name and save files in an organized manner to minimize frustration in the next lesson, when they will import illustrations into PowerPoint in order, according to their storyboards. Encourage students who are confident scanners to assist peers who need help.

As students wait their turn to use the scanner, they should be finishing up their storyboards, using the graphic organizer for comic book creation. At this point, each student should know which text and which illustration will fill each panel. If they have not already titled their stories, now is the time to decide on a title.

On Their Own

Tech Tool Practice: If students are unable to finish scanning illustrations to digital files, they should complete this outside of class.

Creating Digital Comic Books in PowerPoint

During the fifth lesson, students will create their comic books in PowerPoint. They will import their digital illustrations and copy and paste text from the Word document of their stories.

Objectives

Teaching

The instructor will:

- Demonstrate the use of PowerPoint, including importing illustrations and copying and pasting text from Word

- Encourage students who understand PowerPoint well to coach their peers

- Explain how students will use their finished graphic organizer for comic book creation to guide their work in PowerPoint

Learning

Students should understand:

- How to import illustration files and copy and paste text in PowerPoint

- How to use their finished graphic organizer for comic book creation to guide their work in PowerPoint

Lesson Description

Demonstrate the use of PowerPoint. One PowerPoint slide should equal one panel from the graphic organizer for comic book creation. Show students how to import their illustration files, one per slide, according to their graphic organizers for comic book creation. Also demonstrate how to copy text from their stories in Word and paste text onto each slide. Demonstrate the text formatting functions of PowerPoint, such as bold, underline, changing fonts, and changing text color. Discuss how the text and the illustrations can work together to tell the story.

Students will now open a blank slide deck in PowerPoint and begin importing illustrations and copying and pasting text out of Word. Remind students to save their work often. Encourage students who understand the process well to assist their peers.

On Their Own

Tech Tool Practice: If students are unable to finish their comic books during class time, they should finish their work outside of class.

Presentation Practice: Students should practice presenting their comic books to their peers. Let students know what you'll be looking for as they present.

Presenting Digital Comic Book to Peers

During the sixth lesson, students will, one by one, present their finished digital comic books to their peers, using the interactive whiteboard. They will explain why they chose the storyline they did, how they chose which plot points to illustrate, and the choices they made with text placement and formatting. Peers will be encouraged to offer positive feedback and to ask questions.

Objectives

Teaching

The instructor will:

- Remind students of the elements of a good presentation (such as practice, eye contact, clear speaking voice)

- Encourage students to offer positive feedback on presentations and to ask questions

Learning

Students should understand:

- The elements of a good presentation (such as practice, eye contact, clear speaking voice)

- How to explain the choices they made in creating their comic books to their audience

Lesson Description

One by one, students present their digital comic books to their peers. This may be done using an interactive whiteboard or a screen projector; in a small class, students may gather around a computer. The student should first step through each panel of the comic book slowly, allowing the audience to read and appreciate the story. Then, the student should step through each panel again, explaining his or her choices in plot, illustrations, and text placement and formatting. Peers should be encouraged to offer positive feedback and to ask questions.

Appendix A

SPECIAL EDUCATION IN NEW YORK CITY

T he New York City Department of Education (NYCDOE) is home to more than 1.1 million students (http://schools.nyc. gov/AboutUs). The NYCDOE provides academic supportive services to the almost 138,000 students classified with disabilities. However, of this number, approximately 23,000 students receive part or all of their education and services away from the general student population in District 75 (D75), the citywide self-contained division for the severely disabled. D75 consists of 56 school organizations, home and hospital instruction, and vision and hearing services. The schools and programs are located at more than 350 sites in the Bronx, Brooklyn, Manhattan, Queens, Staten Island, and Syosset, New York. The mission of D75 is to provide appropriate standards-based educational programs, with related service supports, to students with severe challenges, commensurate with their abilities. Based on the No Child Left Behind (NCLB) policy, the Individuals with Disabilities Act (IDEA), and curriculum standards, "highly qualified" teachers are mandated to prepare the student population academically, with the use of technology as an instructional tool, for the changing educational, technological, economic, and financial times.

The IDEA defines an individual with disability as having mental retardation; hearing, vision, speech, orthopedic, or language impairment; or serious emotional disturbance, autism, traumatic brain injury, specific learning disorders, deafness, deaf-blindness, multiple disabilities, and other health impairments (IDEA, 2004, section 602). However, IDEA states a person is not defined by his or her disability, rather it should be considered a characteristic of his or her person. Therefore, the law guarantees a child with a disability should be served in a regular classroom with as much interaction with his or her non-disabled classmates as possible. A child with a disability may only be removed from the regular classroom when the nature or severity of the disability is such that the education in regular classes cannot be achieved satisfactorily, even with the use of supplementary aids and services. For example, a child with a speech disability may appropriately be educated in most academic areas in the regular classroom, but it may be necessary to remove the child from the classroom to work in small groups or one-on-one, specifically in the area of reading.

Students classified with a disability are educated based on their Individualized Educational Plan (IEP). The IEP, a legal document, stipulates the educational criteria (setting, goals, and modification), types of additional support services (counseling, occupational therapy), and assessments the student must receive. In New York City, students in D75 self-contained classes are classified into two educational strands—Standardized Assessment or Alternate Assessment—based on the severity of their disability. The Committee on Special Education (CSE), including the student when appropriate, and the student's parents/family/guardians, make these educational and supplementary support decisions. Standardized Assessment classes are generally 12:1:1 or the more restrictive 8:1:1 setting—12 or 8 students, 1 teacher, and 1 paraprofessional. The students assigned to these academic settings are considered to be capable of taking the New York State Standardized Examinations (with testing accommodations) as the general education population. The academic program for the Standardized students is geared toward earning a regular high school diploma. Alternative Assessment classes are generally 12:1:4 and 6:1:1 to accommodate students with multiple disabilities (such as mental retardation, blindness, and orthopedic impairment).

According to the NYCDOE's website, Alternate assessment students also classified with multiple disabilities are also known as "multiply-challenged." This classification refers to a student with concomitant impairments, such as mental retardation and blindness, or mental retardation and orthopedic impairment. These combinations may cause educational needs that cannot be accommodated in a standardized special education program solely for one of the impairments. Most students with multiple disabilities are educated in 12:1:4 classrooms (12 students, one teacher, and four paraprofessionals) or 6:1:1 classrooms.

PS/MS South Bronx is located in the students' home community, the South Bronx. It is a high poverty area. According to the 2007–08 schools' report card (New York City Department of Education, 2008, www.nystart.gov/publicweb), this D75 school is attended by more than 370 students of poverty-stricken or working-class families. The student population in 2008 was 70% Hispanic and 30% African American. The gender breakdown was 60% male and 40% female, which is a typical gender composition of most urban special education school settings in New York City. The annual attendance rate was about 84%, which is below the city average of 90%.

Poverty, disability, and high incidences of absences are factors affecting these students' academic abilities. According to the United States Census Bureau population profile, the presence of a disability is associated with lower levels of income and an increased likelihood of being in poverty. IDEA (1997) reported that poor students of color are two to three times more likely than their white counterparts to be identified by their teacher as having emotional disorders or mental disabilities.

As an educator, I must recognize each student's ability, disability, needs, and desires to learn. I cannot let their personal circumstances or labeling shape my willingness to learn about them or to teach them. Rather, I must acknowledge who they are and their personal cultural accessories they bring with them to the educational environment. Knowing the students will enable me to tailor an academic and social setting that would allow them to access material. Lave and Wenger (1991) believe learning is a situated activity in sociocultural practices of a community and is a relationship between newcomers and experienced individuals. Serioux Comix, a smaller space within the larger school, was intentionally designed as a learning community of practice that was free of social labels. It was a space that was rich academically, technologically, and socially and one that empowered all members regardless of their disability classification, social backgrounds, or academic deficiencies.

Appendix B

*R*ESOURCES FOR *EDUCATORS*

Guide to Comic Books in Education

Althoug this book is meant to be a guide for implementing a Serious Comix project, it is not the only guide available to educators who wish to bring comics into the classroom. Teachers may find the following guide helpful.

Comic Book Project
www.comicbookproject.org

> The Comic Book Project is a well-established arts-based literacy and learning initiative. It is designed to help students write, design, and publish original comics. This project is also designed to help teachers integrate comics into their existing curricula.

Comic Book Creation Software

Comic Life 2
http://plasq.com

> Comic Life 2 is a free digital storyboard creation software. All elements of a comic are available in a drag-and-drop interface: layout templates, speech balloons, captions, lettering, and more. Users can import digital photos and graphics.

Comic Book Creator
http://download.cnet.com/Comic-Book-Creator-Standard/3000-6675_4-10461623.html

> Comic Book Creator is a self-publishing toolkit for making photo comics or classic comics from scanned artwork or video game screenshots.

Graphics Software

Gimp
www.gimp.org

> Gimp is freely distributed software that is used to manipulate images. Users can retouch photos, compose and construct images, and more.

Inkscape
http://inkscape.org

> Inkscape is an open-source graphics editor. Its functionality is similar to that of Adobe Illustrator.

Productivity Software

Google Docs
http://docs.google.com

> Google offers a suite of free software applications, including Google Documents (a word processor) and Google Slides (similar to PowerPoint).

OpenOffice
http://OpenOffice.org

> This is a free, open-source office productivity software suite that includes word processing, spreadsheets, presentations, graphics, and databases.

REFERENCES

Arizpe, E. (2001). "Letting the story out": Visual encounters with Anthony Browne's *The Tunnel*. *Reading: Literacy and Language, 35*(3),115–119.

Barton, P. E., & Jenkins, L. (1995). *Literacy and dependency: The literacy skills of welfare recipients in the United States.* Princeton, NJ: Educational Testing Service.

Bausell, C. V. (2008). Tracking U.S. trends: States vary in classroom access to computers and in policies concerning school technology. *Education Week, 27*(30). Retrieved from www.edweek.org/ew/articles/2008/03/27/30dsr.h27.html

Bay, M. & Bryan T. (1992). Differentiating children who are at risk for referral from others on crucial classroom factors. *Remedial and Special Education, 13*(4) 27–33.

Bloom, B. S. (1984). *Taxonomy of educational objectives: The classification of educational goals.* New York, NY: Longman.

Boyle, J. R., & Weishaar, M. (1997). The effects of expert-generated versus student- generated cognitive organizers on the reading comprehension of students with learning disabilities. *Learning Disabilities Research & Practice, 12*(4), 228–235.

Coley, R. J., & Barton, P. E. (2006). Locked up and locked out: An educational perspective on the U.S. prison population. Educational Testing Service: Princeton, NJ. Retrieved from www.ets.org/research/policy_research_reports/publications/report/2006/dbcz

Collins, R. (2004). *Interaction ritual chains.* Princeton, NJ: Princeton University Press.

Daiute, C. (1983). *Writing and computers.* Reading, MA: Addison-Wesley.

Drakeford, W. (2003). The impact of an intensive literacy program to increase the literacy skills of youth confined in juvenile corrections. *Journal of Correctional Education, 23,* 32–42.

Gunning, T. (2003). *Creating literacy instruction for all children* (4th ed.). Boston, MA: Allyn and Bacon.

Individuals with Disabilities Act. (1997). Retrieved from www.cec.sped.org/law_res/doc/law/index.php

Individuals with Disabilities Education Improvement Act. (2004). Pub. L. 108-446 U.S.C.

International Reading Association. (2000). *Making a difference means making it different: Honoring children's rights to excellent reading instruction* [Position statement]. Newark, DE: Author.

Lave, J., & Wenger, E. (1991). *Situated learning: Legitimate peripheral participation.* Cambridge, UK: Cambridge University Press.

Lenhart, A., Rainie, L., & Lewis, O. (2001). *Teenage life online* [Research report]. Washington, DC: Pew Internet & American Life Project.

Marshall, J. M. (2002). *Learning with technology: Evidence that technology can, and does, support learning.* San Diego, CA: Cable in the Classroom.

Marzano, R. J., Pickering, D. J., & Pollock, J.E. (2001). *Classroom instruction that works: Research-based strategies for increasing student achievement.* Alexandria, VA: Association for Supervision and Curriculum Development.

Mink, J. S. (1988, March). *Integrating reading, writing, and learning theory: A method to our madness.* Paper presented at the Annual Meeting of the Conference on College Composition and Communication, St. Louis, MO. (ERIC Document Reproduction Service No. ED294166)

Moore, D. W., & Readence, J. E. (1984). A quantitative and qualitative review of graphic organizer research. *Journal of Educational Research, 78*(1), 11–17.

Ngao, J. (2006). *Visual classroom.* Retrieved January 2, 2010 from www.lexisnexis.com.libaccess.fdu.edu

No Child Left Behind Act (NCLB) (2001). Washington, DC: U.S. Department of Education. Retrieved from www2.ed.gov/nclb/landing.jhtml

Parsad, B., & Jones, J. (2005). *Internet access in U.S. public schools and classrooms: 1994–2003* (NCES 2005-015). U.S. Department of Education. Washington, DC: National Center for Education Statistics.

Peck, K., & Dorricott, D. (1994). Why use technology? *Educational Leadership, 51*(7), 11–14.

Piro, J. M. (2002). The picture of reading: Deriving meaning in literacy through image. *Reading Teacher, 56*(2), 126–134.

Roth, W. -M., & Tobin, K. (2002). *At the elbow of another: Learning to teach by coteaching.* New York, NY: Peter Lang.

Roth, W. -M., & Tobin, K. (2004). Cogenerative dialoguing and metaloguing: Reflexivity of processes and genres. *Forum Qualitative Sozialforschung/Forum: Qualitative Social Research, 5*(3), Article 7. Retrieved from www.qualitative-research.net/fqs-texte/3-04/04-3-7-e.htm

Rowe, M. B. (1972). *Wait-time and rewards as instructional variables. Their influence in language, logic, and fate control.* Paper presented at the National Association for Research in Science Teaching, Chicago, IL.

Sani, R. (2007). *Creative means to bridge old and new teaching.* Retrieved January 2, 2010 from www.lexisnexis.com.libaccess.fdu.edu

Sewell, W. H. (1999). The concept(s) of culture. In V. E. Bonnell & and L. Hunt (Eds.), *Beyond the cultural turn: New directions in the study of society and culture* (pp. 35–61). Berkeley, CA: University of California Press.

Short, K. G., Shroeder, J., Laird, J., Kauffman, G., Ferguson, M. J., & Crawford, K. M. (1996). *Constructing knowledge together: Classrooms as centers of inquiry and literacy.* Portsmouth, NJ: Heinemann.

Starr, L. (2004). *Eek! Comics in the classroom!* Retrieved from www.educationworld.com/a_purr/profdev/prfodev105.shtml.

Tobin, K., & Roth, W.-M. (2006). *Teaching to learn: A view from the field.* Rotterdam, Netherlands: Sense Publishers.

Tomlinson, C. A. (2001). *How to differentiate instruction in mixed-ability classrooms* (2nd ed.). Alexandria, VA: ASCD.

Wenger, E. (1999). *Communities of practice. Learning, meaning and identity.* Cambridge, UK: Cambridge University Press.

Wilson, W. J. (1996). *When work disappears: The world of the new urban poor.* New York, NY: Knopf.